One Hour Guide to:
New Business Startup

A Simplified Guide to Starting Your First Business

DEVELOP YOUR ENTREPRENEURSHIP

ARTHUR FOSS

Manufactured in the United States of America.

Library of Congress Cataloging-in-Publication Data

2019919188

Foss, Arthur

One Hour Guide to New Business Startup:

A Simplified Guide to Starting Your First Business / Arthur Foss

ISBN 978-0-578-63162-2

LCCN 2019919188

First Edition

One Hour Guide to New

Business Startup

A Simplified Step by Step Guide to Starting Your First Business

DESCRIPTION

As a how to book *One Hour Guide to New Business Startup,* will provide information, direction and motivation on starting your own first business. *One Hour Guide to New Business Startup* is designed for those with limited free time, those looking for condensed but pertinent, subject specific information and presented in an easy to read no non-sense format. Starting your first business, be it home based, brick and mortar or a Franchise the procedure can be daunting. *One Hour Guide to New Business Startup* will take you through the process step by step, without all the hyperbole and rhetoric associated with starting a business.

The objective of the book is to not see if you can read it in an hour, but to allow you to read through and absorb the contents utilizing what pertains to your specific situation and needs and hopefully asking you to set aside an hour to concentrate on one subject.

/////////////////////

The *One Hour Guide* series provides a wide variety of topics; Public Speaking, Time Management, Entrepreneurship and life after school, to name a few. Designed to not take up a lot of your time, but to give you the essentials of the topic you're interested in. Today's world, be it school, relationships or work seems to come at us at a racers pace. By taking One Hour of your time, and leaving the rest of the world outside, to immerse yourself in a subject that could positively enhance your being and may make all the difference as to how you handle life's experiences.

TABLE OF CONTENTS

CHAPTERS

CHAPTER 1

INTRODUCTION

ENTREPRENEURSHIP

The ultimate Guide for the First Time Business Owner

EN-TRE-PRE-NEUR, a noun, and according to Oxford Dictionaries, a person who organizes and operates a business or businesses, taking on greater than normal financial risks in order to do so.

When you think of an Entrepreneur the first people that may come to mind might be Jeff Bezos (Amazon), Bill Gates (Microsoft) or possibly Mark Zuckerberg (Facebook). Believe it or not they all started out with just an idea, so can you. Whether you're thinking of becoming the next Billionaire or just wanting to start that small business to give you that freedom of being your own boss and taking control of your life, it all starts out the same – an idea, the desire to make it happen and the determination to see it through.

In the real-world Entrepreneurs are not just the ones who want to start their own businesses, they are also those that are always looking for new and more efficient and better ways to make a business or organization run more successful and profitable. They may not be nationally recognized or become Millionaires but with-in their personal realm of associates they will be seen as the one who thought outside the box and wasn't afraid to make it known. These too are Entrepreneurs.

Let's take a minute and see if we can try to explain that Entrepreneurial spirt. I believe somewhere deep down in all of our DNA's is that little Genome that creates the Entrepreneurial spirit. So how does it all start, I think it goes something like this; on any given day, your mind is doing it's normal thing: your walking, talking, breathing and hopefully your heart is beating, then with really not knowing it you see, hear or do something that causes two little brain cells to slam into each other and that little Genome starts a seedling of an idea. Then as it is nurtured with imagination, innovation, and creativity it starts to sprout into a full-fledged idea. Until at some point when it is verbalized and brought out into the light of day as a conscious thought, that's when the ENTREPRENEUR thing kicks in.

It wasn't always as easy as it is today. Back in the day when Kings and Emperors and Omnipotent potentates ruled the land, if your father was a baker, a cobbler or a blacksmith, you were expected to follow in the family trade, and ladies your options were extremely limited, your best hope was to marry a wealthy gentlemen. Once the new world (America) was discovered, settled and Constitutionalized proclaiming that we were a free society, the door to Entrepreneurship was flung wide open. People were no longer bound by the century old European mantra, but now they could follow their hearts, and dreams in whatever direction it took them.

When the Industrial Revolution, took place it was a mecca for not only the industrial brain children like Henry Ford and John D Rockefeller but for fledgling Entrepreneurs who would follow, opening support businesses following the lead and the needs of the mega Industrialists. Individuals that would take their own ideas and make businesses, producing goods and services that would enhance the lives of everyone and provide an income for them and their families. It has manifested itself into what opportunities we see today, where it is not only equipment, products and services, but intangibles like Web sites, software, and social media, the possibilities became numerous and endless. Gender, race, nationality or social status play no part in developing that

Entrepreneurial spirit, if you think you have what it takes, think about it, talk about it and write it down then go for it.

There is more to starting a business than just opening your

This book is not intended to take you from cradle to grave in your business, because every business is unique, but a lot of the moving parts are generic and with this basic outline for starting your own business you should be able to build that basic foundation for that initial startup. Then as your business develops you will have the satisfaction of knowing that you have a solid foundation to build on enabling you to make adjustments that will move you in to successful business ownership.

Before we get started let me leave you with this thought for the day:

*If you think you can, you **can** – if you think you **can't** for sure you can't*

CHAPTER 2

<u>WHAT THEY DIDN'T TEACH YOU IN SCHOOL</u>

I am going to say that most of you out there have at least a high school education, many more of you have attended some form of college, and a lot of you have attained degrees, even masters and doctorates. God bless you if you have any or all of these. But all the education you could ever achieve is useless if you haven't found a way to apply it in the real world.

Our public-school systems are mandated to teach a basic curriculum, reading, writing, (any more they have stopped teaching cursive, so you may not really know how to "write") and arithmetic. I remember in my senior year of high school I only had two required classes, some kind of social studies and a P.E. class. I wonder why they didn't throw in some classes on how to balance a check book, how to write a resume or how to conduct yourself in an interview or even better how to begin looking for a job. After all, not everyone is going to go to college.

Should College be your choice and you are embarking on a 4-year journey to a degree, look ahead to what career path you are going down. Ask yourself what degree will be needed to get that position and will it pay enough to repay my educational costs, as well as give me the income needed to live the lifestyle your accustomed too.

I was having dinner not to long ago with a friend who is a very successful business owner. Our server came over to take our order, a young lady who had that college student look about her. My friend asked her if she was attending college, she replied "yes I am, I'm going for a degree in Fine Art." My friend, being the realest he is asked, "and how do you plan to make a living?" She was taken somewhat aback but replied "and what would you like to order."

Don't get me wrong any kind of formal education and/or a college degree will help you get ahead in the business world, even if you do not work in the field you have your degree in, which is usually the case. Employers like to hire people who have demonstrated they had the determination to complete a 4-year education. But think about it, whether it is a small business or a major corporation, you may wind up working for, someone somewhere had to have an idea and the vision to take that leap of faith to go out on his or her own and start that business. And those with less than a high school education, top the list of Entrepreneurial new business startups. Who knew?

If College is not right for you, but you are still looking for more education, Vocational Schools or Community Colleges may be just the answer. There are a multitude of these schools with programs ranging from; Mechanic's, Welding and A/C repair, to all types of Medical applications, Computer Science and Business practices just to name a few.

The Military is another source of "free" education. Not everyone in the Military is a "foot soldier" they also will teach you to be a Pilot, or an aircraft repairman, work in the Medical field, Computer Sciences, or any number of career opportunities applicable to the civilian world. They also offer financial assistance towards a College education, after your out of the service.

Most first-time entrepreneurs rely a lot on self-education, and will search out classes or training, whether it's online or a traditional class format, to focus on what it is they need to know to operate their business.   Owning your own business is an ongoing educational experience and even though you may not have that sheep skin to hang on your wall, you will have that same sense of accomplishment long after "graduation day."

Education in whatever form is a valuable tool to the Entrepreneur,

along with that entrepreneurial spirit flowing through your veins and that drive and determination to succeed is what will take you to your dreams.

. *BEING EDUCATED IS DIFFERENT THAN BEING SMART*

CHAPTER 3

BUSINESS PERSONALITY

As a rule, those of you with that Entrepreneurial spirit to begin with, tend to have that "A" type personality from the start. You are thought of as being strong minded, aggressive and a focused individual. And to some extent that may be true, but if you have the passion for whatever it is you are about to start, you will see these traits raise to the surface. Your personality plays a big part in how your business starts and runs, your personality effects the company's policies & procedures, your hiring and firing practices as well as Customer Service.

Your personal personality may not be the same as your business personality: the way you conduct yourself with family and friends is not always the same as when you are in the business environment. As a business owner you will be required to wear many hats, one of which is knowing when to take off that business hat and replace it with that Family, Friends and social hat.

I'm sure that many of you have taken a personality test in the course of your careers, but just for some quick insight, go to www.personalitytype.com . This is a 4 question personality specific test, it is only between you and yourself, so be honest; you may find it interesting to take the test again in a few months after you have opened your business to see if your personality profile has changed.

Personality traits of a successful Entrepreneur:

o **A passion for what you do or sell.**

Be excited to tell anyone and everyone about your business in a manner that gets them excited as well.

o **Self-disciplined**.

Be self-aware and stay focused, make good solid business decisions and avoid knee jerk reactions to situations.

- **Self-motivated**. Don't be afraid to give yourself a pep talk now and then, look past those bumps in the road and keep your eyes on the goal post.

- **Resourceful**. Avail yourself of every and all opportunities to gather as much information as possible about running your business.

- **Ability to work well with people.** Employees, Customers, Suppliers, Vendors ETC. They are all people so put on your happy face and develop those relationships

- **A desire to be independent**. Being an independent thinker qualifies you as being independent, you may be inundated with advice, recommendations and information, remember you need to think independently as to what is best for your business.

- **A sense of humor.** It's important that you see the humorous side of things, business situations that may seem disastrous at first, will many times, as you look back become very funny.

- **No shrinking violet.** You do not have to be the center of attention but never shy away from a conversation or opportunity to promote your business.

- **Ability to make a plan and see it through**. Successful Entrepreneurs know the value of a plan (a road Map) with milestones so they know where they are on their travels to their final destination.

- **Not afraid to ask for help.** Starting a new endeavor is a challenging task, and the diverse facets of business ownership are numerous, help is out there do not be afraid to ask.

As you evaluate these traits, be honest with yourself, know where

your strong points are and which ones you are going to need to work on. Many people have great management skills and are very organized and focused, while others are more people oriented. The successful business owner will find a way to blend these all together. Taking a realistic look at your abilities is key to having your business run smoothly and grow. It goes without saying if you have great management and organizational skills you will probably need to hire a People person, and vice versa if you're great with people find a great operations manager. If in fact you prefer to work behind the scenes then hiring the right people to operate the business is crucial, but as the owner it then becomes your responsibility to provide leadership, guidance and direction to assure that your employees are doing their best to keep the business moving ahead as per your vision.

Before starting up that new business, buying an existing business or purchasing a Franchise, do a little due diligence. The following 10 questions have no right or wrong answers, they are primarily designed to get you thinking about some of the very basics of business ownership.

THE TOP TEN QUESTIONS TO ASK YOURSELF BEFORE GOING INTO BUSINESS

1) Why am I starting this business?

   This is a question you need to ask yourself up front and think of it as a long-term commitment.

2) Check to see if anyone is willing to buy your product or service?

Check out the competition, can you compete, is your product or service better, cheaper, or more creative than your competition? Or will you be unique in your industry.

3) Do you have a basic business plan?

It needs to be written down. The what, when, where and how and the goals you will be looking to meet.

4) Will you need.

Employees, equipment, vehicles or special licenses All key factors to startup.

5) Do you have the background?

Do you have the expertise to run the business? Don't be afraid to ask for help or take classes.

6) How will you fund the business?

This is a major concern as your living expenses will probably continue on, as well as the cost of running your business. As a rule, new businesses do not generate a lot of income in the beginning. Plan ahead.

7) What legal structure will you use for your business?

Most small businesses start out as a Sole Proprietor, but as your business grows you may find it necessary to change that structure, always get some legal advice on what structure works best for you.

8) <u>Are you committed?</u>

This is a serious question and it requires an honest answer from you, are you willing to give the time, the effort and the money it takes to make your business a success?

9) <u>Do you have the support?</u>

Is your significant other, family and friends, behind you, as it will affect their lives as well as well as yours.

10) <u>Do you have a backup plan?</u>

Not every business makes it. Be prepared to move on, should

the unthinkable happen.

Let me just say that your personality is reflected in your business. Depending on the business you have and the interaction you have with customers, you will have to decide where you best fit in. You may well be the one out front, or there again you may be better suited for managing and running the operation from behind the scene. This is one of the decisions you as the owner must make, it may not be at the outset but somewhere along the line you will have to decide.

Personalities are a strange thing, they are not tangible, so they are not easily manipulated, and being what they are they will have a definite effect on people's perception of not only you but your company as well.

CHAPTER 4

BUSINESS PLANS

"Failure to plan is a plan to Fail."

This may not be the most exciting part of starting a business, but it is without a doubt a crucial part of the puzzle. Your Entrepreneurial spirit is in full stride, with ideas flying in all directions and the "let's get rolling" can't wait to get out the gate. As with any adventure or road trip you need that road map, in the business world it is called the Business Plan.

I am not going to give you specifics on how to write your business plan, as your business plan will vary dependent on the type, size and structure of your business. Go to your favorite browser and type in "business plans" or try SBA.GOV you will find plans for every business situation. Or if you don't want to be that sophisticated grab a yellow note pad and follow the list below to get you started. But I will provide you with a generic version of the purpose of the plan, layout and content and why you really need it.

A few things you need to keep in mind when starting to write up your plan.

<u>Write down your thoughts</u> – the memory is a wonderful thing, although it is not infallible, always keep a note pad and pen handy, as you may have that key advertising line or something that will add value

to the company or remembering that one thing you absolutely need to do,

Resources in Business Planning – As you start through the procedure take advantage of all the sources available to you. There are several online as well as the **Small Business Administration** to give you guidance. You may have to adjust your Plan according to how you will start your business; if you are a Sole Proprietor and self-funded your plan will be relatively simple and will basically be a reference tool for you, if you are looking for partners or investors your plan will need to be a little more in-depth, and should you be looking for start-up capital the 4 basic financial statement, Income Statement, Balance Sheet, Cash Flow Statement and Budget are all important to a lending institution and should be put together by a knowledgeable account.

Describe the Business – This is an essential part of the Business Plan, by writing down a description of your business you have now put some thought into what your vision of the company really is, what will the company actually do, who will be your customers, what service or product will you supply and how will you fit into that market.

What is your Market and Marketing Plan – Write a short paragraph

23

about the Market you are getting into, and what is your sales and marketing plan to penetrate that market.

<u>Below are 6 basic items to organize your plan</u>:

<u>Mission Statement</u> – a basic statement of why the business was started and what you hope to attain.

<u>Objectives</u> – put together some realistic milestones you want to accomplish, with dates. This can be done on a daily, weekly or monthly basis.

<u>Goals</u> – Look to the future, long term, to give yourself a target to shoot for, and get that feeling of accomplishment when you reach it. Goals like number of sales or jobs performed, income objectives and market penetration.

<u>Organization</u> – How will your company be structured, Owner(s) Management, employees making sure all are aware of their positions and duties and goals of the company.

<u>Procedures</u> – a policy and procedures book, even if it is very informal in the beginning is very important, so that all know what is acceptable as far as dress, language and

customer service, you also want it stated what is not acceptable.

Personnel – in the beginning it may be only you, but as your company grows, you will need to know what skill sets the people you hire will need. Thinking about this ahead of time not only prepares you for the future but makes you aware of what you need to know as well.

Let's be serious, most of us are in it for the money. In your business plan there needs to be a place to discuss finances, Initial startup costs, Company operating costs, expected company income remembering all the time you will still have your everyday living expenses and. Most Entrepreneurs are great doers and come up with great ideas but are not always at the top of their game when it comes to the day to day obligation of operations and bookkeeping. That being said, in the beginning finding a close family member or friend to do the books, if you are unable to do them yourself, is probably in your best interest. But before long you will need to find an Accountant who can produce professional accounting documents and keep you on good terms with the IRS and local tax agencies.

BUSINESS PLAN CHECK LIST

Below are 11 items to help you format your business plan. Take each item individually and write a few lines to define that subject, as time goes by you can go back and add, subtract or adjust your initial thoughts to fit the current status of your company.

1. Company Overview – give a brief description of the Company itself.

2. Ownership – if you are starting out as a Sole Proprietor say so.

3. Management & Organization – explain Management & how the Company will operate.

4. Goals & Objectives – be specific as to what you want to accomplish and by what date. Break it into 90-day cycles to better see results and to allow for adjustments.

5. Product or Service – describe in depth your product or service.

6. Marketing - describe in detail what is your advertising program and when and how will you begin it.

7. Sales –Sales, will you accept Credit Cards, checks, or cash, explain. How will you sell, online, over the counter, service work orders, will you offer terms and billing.

8. Pricing – show each product or service retail price, will you sell wholesale or offer discounts, be sure this is laid out on a price sheet, one retail one wholesale.

9. Competitors – list your competitors and explain how you will compete against them

10. Expenses & Startup Costs – list one-time Initial costs, ongoing Monthly expenses, Payroll, inventory & operating supplies.

11. Action Plan – Start date, get legal, Marketing, lay out 1st 90 days.

This may not be everything you need for your business plan as it will vary dependent on the size of your company, the company structure, the type of business you are conducting and if you are looking for funding. None of this is cast in stone, and you may need to modify your Plan as time goes on, but keep in mind when your first starting out, this plan is your benchmark and all changes will grow from this document.

CHAPTER 5

STARTING UP

I'm not big on numbers and statistics, and the numbers you see below are outdated (the Census Bureau only does this every 10 years) today the numbers are considerably higher. More and more people are moving away from a "job" and are looking to take charge of their lives and not be subject to layoffs, downsizing and re-organization. Take a look below and you will get an idea of the family of Entrepreneurs you will be joining as you begin your quest for business ownership

According to the US Census Bureau "2011."

- There are 28 Million small businesses in the US.

- 22 million, or nearly 75%, of those are Self Employed or "nonemployer" type businesses. (meaning they have no employees.)

- 7.8 million are owned by Woman (28.7 percent of all businesses Nationwide).

- Approximately 543,000 NEW businesses start up each month

- Over 50% of small businesses are **home based.**

- **Sole Proprietorships**, 19.4 million, make up the majority of Small Businesses, **Partnerships** are 1.6 million

- **Corporations.** are 1.4 million
- **The average annual income for a self-employed business owner is $44,000 annually.**

So why is it that you think people want to start their own businesses? Many want to start a business because they want that feeling of independence, that feeling of being in control of their own destiny. Others see a need that is not being filled and move forward to fill it. Many others fall into it as part of a Family owned Business or are forced into starting their own business because maybe their employer is downsizing, laying-off, or is being bought out, or through the re-organization of a department or a position has been eliminated.

Think about the businesses you are involved with every day; your

hairdresser, barber, plumber, landscaper, house cleaner, insurance agent, physical therapist, or a house painter just to name a few. This is just a small segment of the over 22 million Self Employed businesses. So, if you are seriously thinking about joining the ranks of the Self Employed, keep this one word in mind **"OWNER."** Unlike when you are an employee and have a "job" and you can look forward to that paycheck, and quitting time, and that vacation you schedule every year. As the "owner," even though you have closed the business for the day, in the back of your mind you will be thinking of all the myriad of things that still need to be done, and there will be those long unpaid overtime hours making sure your business is up and running. But then that is all part of the joy of business ownership.

In a later chapter we will go more in depth into types of Business Ownership, such as Sole Proprietor, Partnerships, purchasing an existing Business or a Franchise. But for the time being let's look into you personally. As a new Entrepreneur do you have that enthusiasm and drive to take that leap of faith and take that road less traveled on into the new and exciting adventure known as Business Ownership.

If you think you have what it takes, now is a great time to start your own business. Get those creative juices flowing, Men, Women, Minorities and even you young adults, new business startups are at its highest rate in over 20 years. But before you fly off into to the ibis you have got to have a good business foundation, starting with a business plan (even if it is only one you hand wrote on the back of a napkin at the kitchen table) by writing your plan down and verbalizing it, it becomes a starting point for you to build on.

A Quick Thought for The Day

"FAILURE TO PLAN IS A PLAN TO FAIL."

Nationwide 543 Thousand new solo owned businesses start up every Month (according to the SBA), if you take a look at that number you might ask yourself is there room for one more. The answer is **YES!** But the success or failure of your business will depend on how much homework and preparation you do before opening day. Starting a new business involves planning, how will the business actually operate, making the right financial and Legal decisions for starters. Many startups use business consultants or coaches, if you have never started a business before I would highly recommend this. The SBA (Small Business Administration) is also a great source for new business startup information, and it's for FREE.

Your legal and financial advisors will be there to impart the wisdom that is their expertise, (many of these are small business owners themselves) a good Attorney and CPA will help you put together that foundation so necessary to build your business on.

Regardless of the type of business you start, remember you and you alone are responsible for its success or failure (50% of new start-ups fail,) which means a 24/7/365 commitment from you is essential. Although in reality you won't be alone, you'll have Federal & State governments, City and County Governments and of course the IRS, all helping you run your business. All the more reason to have knowledgeable support people to turn to for advice.

It is interesting to note that at some point in time your business will become an entity in and of itself with its own reputation, community standing and credit worthiness. In the beginning it is important that you keep in mind all your startup business dealings will be based on your personal character, your past work history and personal credit worthiness. As a Small Business owner your income may be reduced and be harder to verify (no pay stubs) which will affect your ability to purchase items on credit based on the business. Some businesses require more start-up capital than others, this is one of the big reasons to put that business plan together right up front. Because it is highly unlikely that a business is profitable right from the get-go.

In the beginning, you will be looking at your business from the inside out, but whenever possible you should take every opportunity that comes your way to talk to other business owners. Join your local Chamber of Commerce, Business Groups in your area and other business Organizations. Business owners as a rule love to talk about their businesses, to other business owners, and you can gather some valuable information and insights from their experiences. They may also be able to steer you around some common pit falls, as well as possibly directing you to finding some good support businesses that can help you manage and grow your business.

We will be discussing a little further on about the various types of

business ownership, financing, and what it takes to actually run a business. So even though each business is unique unto itself, there are always similarities in business in general, so the more you can educate yourself with real world information the better off you will be.

As I researched information for this book it is amazing how many

"theories" are out there on how to start a first-time business, most of them presented by those that have never owned a business, made a payroll, or worked with customers. So, there is nothing wrong with being aware of other ideas, but always look at it through the filter of can that really be applied to my business.

Think about it, once you're up and running, and when someone asks you "what do you do for a living" you can reply without reservation and with that Pride in Ownership, "I own my own Business."

WHAT YOU WILL NEED TO OPEN THE DOORS

DBA or TRADE NAME REGISTRATION – (DBA stands for DOING BUSINESS AS).

These are legal documents, generally issued by your Secretary of State, and it registers your Business Name, the date you started your business, what type of business are you engaged in, and identifies who is the owner.

TPU or TRANSACTION PRIVILEGE/USE TAX LICENSE

This is a State license issued by the States Department of Revenue,

it is what you need to buy product and supplies wholesale (with-out paying taxes and at a discounted Price) you in turn will charge the appropriate tax on goods you sell and you will then pay the State the taxes you have collected. In most States this only applies to products, not to services. Products sold over the internet may also be tax-exempt, it varies State by State, check with your State Treasurer.

EMPLOYER IDENTIFICATION NUMBER

This is a number issued by the Internal Revenue Services and is primarily used by them to identify you and your Business you will use this number when you file your business tax returns. Although in some cases Government Agencies and large Corporations ask that you provide this number. It is very easy to get simply go online to the IRS and apply; there is no cost involved.

BUSINESS CHECKING ACCOUNT

The above-mentioned document (DBA) is required to open a business checking account.

Should you apply for a Business Credit Card, in the beginning it is more than likely going to be based on your personal credit,

LICENSES AND CERTIFICATIONS AND AGREEMENTS

Depending on the type of business you are operating City, County, or State Agencies may require certain special licenses and or certifications to do business in their jurisdictions. Business agreements; Partnerships, Franchise and Lease Agreements should all be in place before moving to far ahead with your opening.

OPERATING CAPITAL

If you are able to continue working, while you start your business, this may well be a big benefit to your startup efforts, as you will find out Cash Flow is crucial to every business. This is one of the big advantages of a Home-Based Business, where you may be able to keep the overhead low while you continue to grow the business. In many cases the startup process is slowed because of trying to do 2 jobs, with your primary income source getting first priority.

We will be talking about finances in a later chapter, but for now dependent on your lifestyle, financial obligations and other sources of income, four to six months of available funds should be set aside to maintain your living expenses. This should be part of your business plan with a realistic picture of what your expenses, both living and business, will look like.

There are many more facets to opening a business, as you continue reading you will find many of the subjects, we touched on here are covered more in depth later on. The startup is a significant part of the business ownership experience and like building a house a strong foundation is key to a successful business. Hence the need for a Business Plan is crucial, no matter how informal it might be.

CHAPTER 6

LET'S TALK FINANCES

Believe it or not it takes money to make money. Although many small businesses can start out on a shoestring, it is not only the cost of starting your business you have to take into consideration, but how are you going to maintain your current living standards and expenses.

I can't express how important a Business Plan is, no matter how informal it is, even if you sit down at your local coffee shop and write it out on a yellow note pad. Do it! Getting something down on paper makes it seem more real, even if you're guessing at some of the numbers you will get a better feeling as to the costs, time commitment and have a road map to profitability.

It is imperative that you have determined just how much money you will need to start and operate your business. Through the use of some type of "spread sheet" broken down to weekly or monthly expenses and expected revenue, you can start tracking your business plans goals and know what adjustments may need to be made.

A little later on we will talk about how and where to borrow money.

But I would like to take a minute and pass on some advice; no matter how good your relationship is and how positive the expectations are on either side, when it comes to money changing hands between family or friends it has been my experience that it never ends well. If you do go this route please get an Attorney involved or at least go on line and get a loan agreement so everyone knows how much was borrowed, how is it going to be repaid, and is it a loan or are they buying into the business. If by lending the money has the lender now become a silent partner, it needs to be written down as to how much input and authority the lender has in the operation of the business. And what happens should the business fail, will they be expecting their investment back, again this needs to be in writing.

Remember when family & friends are involved there is also extended family and friends with their own views on the transaction. It is a slippery slope when money becomes intertwined with relatives or friends.

SELF FUNDING

Let's start close to home, borrowing from your savings should be just that, a loan which you need to repay, this also needs to be done with the approval of your husband, wife or significant other. Tapping into 401K's, retirement or investment accounts can be costly early on with expensive fees and penalties, and if not repaid can severely damage your retirement plans. Your home is another source of non-application lending. Home equity line of credit, a second mortgage, or re-financing, all options that really need to be well thought out before moving ahead. As we talked about above family and friends are another source of funding, but it needs to be treated as a total business arrangement without the relationship aspect, which is really hard to do. As a business arrangement everything needs to be spelled out and agreed to by all parties and signed, preferably drawn up and witnessed by an attorney.

ALTERNATIVE FUNDING

Here are some options on getting startup capital.

VENTURE CAPITAL – Being a first time Entrepreneur and startup Company this may not be your first choice when it comes to new business funding. Beware, first of all, they will want a share of ownership as well as possibly an active role in the operation of the company. As a rule, they are looking for established Companies with low risk, high-growth potential in need of capital in the six-figure range.

ONLINE LENDERS – and there are many, just Google BUSINESS LOANS but once again do your due diligence although they may offer quick funding and are willing to work with those with less than perfect credit and require very little paperwork, keep in mind this comes at a cost. Their interest rates are much higher than traditional loans and their terms are sometimes difficult to understand, and they are noted for their lack of transparency.

CROWDFUNDING – This is an online method of raising capital through social media and crowdfunding platforms. With the crowdfunding approach it gives you the opportunity to present your business model to a large pool of individuals giving them more ways to help grow your business. Google "what is crowdfunding," for more information.

SBA (SBA.GOV).

FYI, the Small Business Administration does not make loans, they work with a variety of lenders, primarily banks. The SBA is however a world of information for small startup companies, with informative and useful links to such items as Starting a business and Managing a business.

BANKS

On a personal level, you have probably been dealing with a bank for years, if so, this may be the right financial institution for you to open your Business checking account in. The first thing you need to do is take your DBA and EIN forms down to your local bank and open a business checking account, this actually tells the world you are officially in business. This is also where your accountant will get a lot of your tax information.

If currently you have your personal banking with a large bank, I would suggest for your business banking you may want to look into working with a smaller local hometown bank or Credit Union.

Although smaller Banks are still guided by the same Rules and Regulations as the big guys you have better access to decision makers and a personal relationship with a banker is never a bad thing.

LEASES & CREDIT CARDS

If you are in need of a short-term loan for say some Equipment financing, most manufactures offer lease programs. These are good options as opposed to a loan as the entire amount of the lease is tax-deductible, where only the interest is deductible on a loan (check with your accountant first). Again as a new business your credit worthiness will be based on your personal credit, and most of the time you will be asked to sign a Personal Guarantee, assuring the lender or lease company that you will be personally responsible for the balance of the loan should the business close.

If you are going to be accepting Credit Cards you will need to set up a Merchants Account, this can be done thru your bank, or other outside credit card processing companies. They all charge for this service, a percentage of the sale. Almost all supply the equipment you will need to swipe the cards, but rates vary, so do some comparison shopping. Try to avoid signing any long-term agreements.

DEALING WITH BANKS

The days of George Bailey (It's a Wonderful Life) are pretty much gone, today all financial institutions are regulated by the Federal

Government and have guidelines they must adhere too. But if a small business loan is in your future here are a few things you need to keep in mind:

Think like a lender – why should they lend you money? You really need to understand your business and be able to explain in detail its operation and why this loan will help you grow.

How much money will you really need – don't try to get more than you really need, be ready to justify why you want the loan and what it will be used for. Once you have made the appointment with the loan officer, be prepared, first of all, put your best foot forward, dress professionally. Be prepared to give the best presentation possible, be excited about your business and demonstrate how this loan will help set your foundation and prepare you for future growth. Understand should the Bank grant you the loan they now have a vested interest in your business and its success, basically you now have an unofficial "partner."

The following are some of the documents and background information you should bring along:

- Personal Resume – to show your work history, management experience, business experience and accomplishments

- <u>Business Plan</u> – this should be in a professional format, reasonably detailed and projected out 3 to 5 years.

- <u>Personal Credit Report</u> – obtain a personal credit report from all three major consumer credit rating agencies.

- <u>Income Tax Returns</u> – Most institutions will ask for the last three years of returns.

- <u>Bank Statements</u> – Generally one year of any and all checking and savings accounts.

- <u>Legal Documents</u> – Business licenses, Certificates, Partnership agreements, other business-related obligations and documentation.

The financing of your business is a major part of the startup process. It's all about commitment, whether you are self-funding, borrowing from family or friends, using alternative funds or doing a business loan ultimately those funds should be dedicated to developing a solid foundation and insuring the growth of your company. To many Small business owners will look at the money in the bank as "theirs" and not think about the financial obligations of the business that must come first. One of the best ways to control this is to pay yourself a salary, now you know exactly how to budget your personal and business expenses.

CHAPTER 7

TYPES OF BUSINESS OWNERSHIP/STRUCTURE

If you think you have what it takes let's see how you will put it all together. The following is a sampling of the types of "business ownership," which means how your business will be set up from a legal standpoint as well as, yes, those pesky IRS guys, from a tax standpoint.

We covered this in an earlier chapter but just to be on the save side we will quickly go over them again here. First decided on a name, then you will need to register that business name with the State. To do so contact your States Secretary of State's office and apply for a **DBA** (Doing Business As license), this registers you with the State as a legitimate business, with this license you will now be able to open a business checking account. There is a very nominal fee for this license. Having this license also allows you to deduct certain business expenses from your State and Federal Income Taxes and purchase goods and services at wholesale prices.

Next you will need to contact the IRS (IRS.GOV.) and get an

EIN

number (Employee Identification Number) this registers you with the IRS, you can do this on line, and the number is used mainly to Identify you as a business rather than an individual, for tax purposes, there is no charge for this. The only other thing you might look into is if there are any City, State or Federal licenses or permits you might need for your type of business. There may also be some local City or State taxes you may be responsible for, always check with your accountant to be sure.

If you will be selling products or parts you will also need a **re-seller's tax license**, this is where you collect the appropriate taxes on each sale, taxes that you didn't pay when you bought the products wholesale, and now it's your turn pay the state their share, although there is no direct cost to you for doing this, should you not pay the sales tax there can be significant fines levied by the State. Your accountant may suggest a separate account for taxes, so as not to comingle those funds. Most States do not charge a tax on Services.

Depending on the type of business you are operating City, County, or State Agencies may require certain **special licenses and or certifications** to do business in their jurisdictions.

Below you will find a short list of types of business ownership, as

always, I recommend you check with a Business Attorney or your Accountant or a Business Consultant as to which structure works best for you.

SOLE PROPRIETOR

If you're doing work for someone and they are paying you for it, WA LA you're a Sole Proprietor or sometimes this is referred to as an Independent Contractor. If you are doing work for another business, they will more than likely report what they paid you to the IRS and will send you a 1099 form (similar to a w-2) for you to use when you file your State and Federal income taxes, as a rule Companies do not take any taxes out of your check. Keep in mind you as a Sole Proprietor are personally responsible, to pay your share of income tax, but business expenses help offset your tax liability, thus the need for a good CPA or Account.

One of the of the downsides of being a Sole Proprietor is that all your assets are at risk should you be sued. Looking into Business Insurance may or may not be a necessity depending on the type of business you are starting, especially if you will be working in people's homes, check with your insurance agent.

As a start -up, if you plan on basically running the business yourself, this is by far the best form of business ownership. As your business grows or you find a need for a partner, you can change to another type of ownership at any time.

PARTNERSHIPS

Anytime two or more people go into business together they have formed a Partnership, this again is a very simple type of ownership. Partnerships should always be in written form! Whether you download it from the web or have an Attorney draw it up, you need to do it. This will describe who is the majority owner, how much and what type of participation each owner has, financial considerations, operational input authority and any and all other considerations related to the business.

Partnerships many times evolve by accident, a person may offer money, or the use of equipment or property, they may bring expertise at no charge or possibly labor. All these may seem like acts of kindness or friendship but as time goes by the giver my assume that by participation, they have earned a partnership relationship. It is best at the outset that you put together an informal form stating that you appreciate their help and support but that it in no way constitutes any type of partnership relationship.

This is all part of the business mentality, always watching out for what is best for your business, what may be a speed bump or what can be an on ramp.

THERE ARE GENERALLY TWO TYPES OF MORE FORMAL PARTNERSHIPS:

LIMITED PARTNERSHIPS - LP

A Limited Partnership differs from other partnerships in that partners are only liable for business debts that do not exceed their initial investment, they are also limited to their input into to the operation of the business by that same initial investment. One of the Partners is designated as the General Partner and is responsible for daily operations and the financials of the company. The LP needs to be registered with the state as a partnership listing all partners their percentage of ownership and submit required documentation as per the Uniform Limited Partnership Act. This is another case of getting an Attorney and/or an account involved early on.

As in any relationship it needs to be clear the responsibility of each participant, when this is put down in written form, any misunderstandings or unspoken assumptions are brought forward from the beginning. Should a partner leave or a new partner come on the agreement needs to be updated immediately.

LIMITED LIABILITY COMPANY – LLC

A Limited Liability Company (LLC) has a similar structure as that of a Corporation whereby the owners are not personally liable for the debts or the liabilities of the Company itself. Because it is a more formal partnership arrangement it does require "articles of organization" and other documentation and it also needs to be registered with the State as an LLC. Owners in the Company are referred to as Members. These documents will also describe the rights, powers, duties, liabilities and other obligations of each Member.

As such the Company, the LLC, does not pay taxes itself, the profits and/or losses are passed on to the personal tax returns of its Members. A couple of disadvantages to an LLC are; should a Member die or file for bankruptcy, depending on the State, the Company may have to be dissolved. LLCs are also not a suitable structure if down the road the Company is looking to be publicly traded. If this sounds like the right vehicle for your endeavor get a qualified business Attorney involved from the outset.

CORPORATION

Corporations give the best protection to its owners shielding them from any personal liability, it is also the most expensive business structure to set up as well as record keeping intensive. The taxing of a corporation is also more involved.

<u>Advantages of forming a Corporation</u>:

Personal asset protection – allows the owners to separate their personal assets.

Additional credibility – "Inc." after your business name gives instant credibility.

Name protection – other business' will not be allowed to file your exact Corp, name.

Perpetual existence – Company continue regardless of owner or management changes.

Tax flexibility – Corporations have options to avoid double taxation.

Expense deductions – the Corporation assumes responsibly for operating expenses.

Investment capital – Investors are more comfortable investing in Corporations.

Disadvantages of forming a Corporation:

Startup costs – Legal and startup costs can be expensive

Documentation – Corp. are documentation intensive, both Federal, State & internally

Loss of control – you will need to answer to a Board of Directors & Share holders

Cumbersome – Size and structure are not conducive to change and direction

These are just a few of the better-known types of entities that are available for business ownership. As a startup once you have decided on the type of business you will be running you will be better prepared to make a decision on what type of business structure is best for you.

CHAPTER 8

OTHER WAYS OF BECOMING A BUSINESS OWNER

You have answered some questions about why you want to become a Business Owner, we have taken a look at the Start Up process and the necessity of business planning as well as the types of business structures. Now let's take a look at some other ways to become a Business Owner.

HOME BASED BUSINESS

Any of you, who while gainfully employed, have had the opportunity to work from home know some of the challenges you'll face if you start a home-based business. Depending on your lifestyle you will have distractions, kids, television, friends, social media, extra-curricular activities, and……. Discipline and focus are key words when it comes to running a business from your home.

All the things we talked about previously still apply, Licenses, DBA, business bank account and so on. Whether you intend to continue to operate out of your home or it's the jumping off point, from the beginning treat it as a BUSINESS. Depending on the type of business you are conducting, if you are going to have people coming in and out of your house, or if you are doing some kind of manufacturing out of your garage, you may want to check with your HOA (if you have one) and/or the City or County to see what regulations or restrictions may pertain to your business.

Many home-based businesses are web oriented, either buying or selling on E bay or Amazon or something similar, which is easy to do from home. You may do accounting, a small boutique, a crafts operation or classes of some sort. Although you may be able to conduct business from the kitchen table, I would heartily suggest that you find a place you can call your office. It will allow you to shift into business mode, and stay focused, it should also be a place where you keep your business paperwork, your customers will also appreciate it should they have a need to come to your "office."

I would suggest you do a little homework first.

Is your house or apartment actually big enough to run a business out of.

Do you have a place to store product, do assembly and shipping?

A place for your computer, printer, files and fax.

Do you have a land line or a dedicated phone number?

Have you checked out the competition?

Are you price competitive?

Will you be able to meet or beat your competitions prices and services?

If you are running a service business, where will you service and park your equipment?

It is also a good thing to remember that even though people want their product at good quality and prices and services done correctly and at a reasonable price, it is also true that people buy people, and developing a rapport with your customers and offering outstanding Customer service will help you with referrals, your business reputation and growth.

Always be as professional as possible, get a business dedicated phone number, which is always answered using the business name and include that in your voice mail box as well. If you get a web page be sure it looks as professional as possible, with enough positive information that the potential customer won't go looking any further. Go online and order business cards, work orders and/or invoices, these are inexpensive and lets your customer know that you are actually in business. It also gives them your contact information to refer you to their friends and neighbors.

BUYING AN EXISTING BUSINESS

Buying an existing business has its pro's and con's and does require that you the buyer do your due diligence. A currently operating business gives you a jump start into business ownership, it gives you instant name recognition, clientele, immediate cash flow and hopefully a good business reputation in the community.

However, do your homework, check to see if the company has any law suits or liens against it, find out if it has any and how much outstanding debt, leases, property or equipment, outstanding equipment loans, or other long term financial obligations, that you may become responsible for.

Don't be afraid to ask why they are selling the business, check their books, ask for bank statements and other financial records, as well as a profit and loss statement. It will be in your best interest to have a 3rd party Business Attorney or CPA take a look at everything. If you do need to assume some of their debt I.E. property lease, operating equipment loans ectara be sure they are in your best interest, if you are planning to make changes to the business some items may not pertain to your new idea. Keep in mind business owner's trying to sell their business will do all they can to make the business look great.

Just for a minute, put aside the excitement of buying the business and step back and take a realistic view, of what the owner is telling you, is what you're seeing what you're getting? Does the number of jobs or customers justify the income they are claiming? Maybe have a friend or relative do a "secret shopper" and get their feedback on their experience. Remember you may be buying the business, but you also are assuming its reputation, customer concept and community awareness. I would be hesitant about making any major changes to the business until you get a feel for the day to day operations.

GOING INTO PARTNERS WITH AN EXISTING BUSINESS.

In an earlier chapter we talked about forming a Partnership business as a startup, buying into or becoming a partner in a currently operating business should be treated similarly to buying an existing business. Your first question should be why do they need a partner? Is there a financial reason behind it? Do they need more help? Do they need your expertise? And what part will you play, will you be a silent partner, a working partner, or just an investor? How much input will you have in the operation of the business? Should you decide to leave the partnership what are the terms and requirements. These are all thing that should be addressed before you sign any agreement.

Be sure to get a good business Attorney review the relationship and draw up the appropriate documents. There is nothing worse than partnering in a business, no matter how well you think you know the individual, with out everything being written out and signed by both parties.

If it looks like a good opportunity and you have lined up those legal ducks, be sure you and everyone else understands what your position is and what and if you have input and /or authority over the operation of the business. Depending on what you have agreed to you may or may not have any authority, you may or may not have any control over finances, Company operation or the businesses direction, all the more reason to have an exit clause in your agreement. It may seem like a great idea in the beginning and it may well be, but should things not go as planned or an unforeseen situation arises you need to have guidelines set up for your departure from the Company.

FRANCHISE

Franchising is basically an established company (franchisor) selling to an individual businessperson (Franchisee) the right to use their name and business model to do business for a fee. That is a very basic explanation, and because of the complexities of the relationship Franchising is regulated by the (FTC) Federal Trade Commission, and the individual states. Before you make the plunge, you need to do your due diligence, understand the Franchisor will probably paint you a pretty rosy picture, so Google it, get a copy of the Uniform Franchise Offering Circular, this contains information on their legal, financial, and personnel history. You may also want to contact other Franchisee's to see how they feel about working with the company.

A significant financial investment is required up front, and as you start to get set up additional investment of time and money more than likely will be required. Another reason for you or your attorney to read the Franchise Agreement thoroughly. Keep in mind with this arrangement you will be giving up some of your Entrepreneurial freedom, as most franchises are very structured. Although the Return on Investment is significant, because their business model is established and successful, compared to other types of businesses, you will be required to conform to the companies operating procedures. The Franchisor has a vested interest in your success, and in the beginning will spend a lot of time making sure you and your employees are up to speed.

Here are a few of the benefits of Franchising.

- Instant name recognition
- Proven business model
- Company Training
- Access to Franchisors approved banks, leasing, insurance, & company software

- Ongoing support

- Advertising assistance

A few of the draw backs are;

- Entrepreneurial spirit may have to be reined in, as you are regulated by the Franchise agreement as to what you are allowed to do.

- A major capital investment at the outset.

- The opportunity to grow and move your business is also restricted.

- Your ability to sell the business is also governed by the terms of the agreement.

- Depending on how you look at it you basically have bought into a partnership.

Franchising is by far the most secure way of going into business, as both parties have a common interest to make the business a success. If you're not sure what type of business to start, there is without a doubt a franchise for almost any business you can think of opening. Be aware of what your signing, have a good business attorney look over the contract and explain to you what your signing. The Franchisor is always going to be looking out for their interests, and you need to know what is expected of you while you are the Franchisee, and should you decide to terminate the relationship can you sell it, close it, or transfer it?

Starting a business on your own is intimidating enough and having someone else there can be very reassuring.

So, whether you're buying a business, going into a partnership relation or a Franchise be sure whatever you do that it is always in your best interest. If for some reason it doesn't feel right, or your having to talk yourself into it, take a moment step back and reevaluate and don't be afraid to step away.

CHAPTER 9

<u>WOMEN and MINORITY'S IN BUSINESS</u>

WOMEN – you are not alone in the business world, the U S Census Bureau reported that in 2012 Nationally there were 9.9 million women-owned businesses, up from 7.8 million in the previous census year in 2007. And since 2016 new business start-ups as a whole, has been growing by leaps and bounds, and Woman and Minorities are a big part of that growth.

There is no doubt starting a business has its own challenges, but for women there are many more life changing decisions that have to be made. Because of the role women play in our social make up, there is an internal struggle that she alone must deal with. And to their credit women seem to have that unique ability to juggle the dual responsibilities of business ownership and her other life.

The young women that are graduating from college, and the twenty somethings, that are thinking towards careers, have some real serious choices to consider. Unlike the days of Ozzie & Harriet and The Brady Bunch where young women were more or less expected to get married and become home makers, or if you did opt to get a job your options were limited to Secretarial, Retail or Waitressing, for the most part, not management or business ownership. But today I don't think woman have ever felt more empowered, whether you have attended college and have gotten your degree, or through hard work and personal accomplishments you have developed that personal sense of self-confidence, you will find now that your options are now unlimited.

As you enter the Work Force or the Corporate environment you will find there will be competition, not only from other women, but men as well, all looking to grasp that holy grail as they work their way up that Corporate ladder. Don't ignore that entrepreneurial spirit, because that is what will inspire you to think outside of the box and make you stand out from the rest of your colleagues. Once you have gained some experience in the real world, you may have found that working in that structured environment is not always what it has cracked up to be, and you may be ready to take that leap of faith and start your own company. Then one day you have gotten the kids off to school, your husband is at work, and you look around and say I really don't want to clean the house again.   That may be a good time to look around at what some of your female friends and neighbors are doing, things like Mary Kay or something similar, or maybe it's another form of business they are running out of their homes. Think about it 9.9 million other women have started and are currently running their own businesses. So why not you.

Regardless of whether you are married, have decided to remain single or are divorced, the opportunity to start your own business is still there. Starting your own business can take on many forms, depending on your aspirations. Keep in mind unlike looking for a job that you might like to do, you can now

find what you really have a passion for and go for it. If you are still undecided about what you might like to do, and you have not been out in the real world for a while, you might think about volunteering. Hospitals, City offices, Schools, Not for Profits are just a few of the places that are always looking for help, this is a great way to start networking and getting a feeling for what might be an opportunity. Another source is the SBA's Office of Women's Business Ownership, as well as the Small Business Administration's general information on small business start-up. The internet can also be a world of information on anything business.

The Census Bureau, God bless their souls, gave us some other interesting facts; nearly 90 percent of women-owned businesses are nonemployers. Which means they have no employees and run the business themselves. Approximately 50 percent of woman owned businesses are in the Health Care, Social Assistance and Educational Services, while the other 50 percent are in what they call Other Services, Crafts, online sales, Tutoring, House Cleaning and Child Care to name a few. You may not think of these as a "business" but in fact they are, and you should think of them as legitimate businesses.

Always present yourself professionally, this doesn't mean you are dressed in a business suit, but it is how you conduct yourself. You should put together a 30 second "speech" so when you meet someone for the first time you a ready to give a professional presentation on you and your business.

Well maybe now those creative juices are starting to flow, it's time to do a little homework. Google your idea in as many forms as you can think of, see how many businesses like the one you're thinking of are out there, go to their web sites see how they operate and how much they charge. The more information you gather before you dive in will help you with your business plan and an overall view of how your business operates as a whole.

If you know someone who has a small business, especially if they operate out of their home, don't be afraid to ask them questions. To know what the day to day challenges are of operating out of your home, will again give you insight as to what you can look forward to and any adjustments you may have to make.

The business world has long known that women tend to be more responsible, dependable and are more likely to complete tasks given to them. They also have found that women are more inclined to be detail oriented, better organized and are more open to new ideas.

These are all attributes associated with whoever is opening a new business. Women starting a new business may have some challenges to meet, that man do not, such as job experience (especially if you married young), Credit background, resume or references and finances/collateral. Even though you might not be thinking of opening a business today, for your own independence; I would suggest opening a savings or checking account in your name, apply for a credit card, use it, but pay it off each month (this will establish your credit score), possibly get a part time job or volunteer to show some work experience.

These are some of the things that help establish you in the business world. Should you need supplies or merchandise to operate your business wholesalers and vendors are more likely to extend you credit terms if you already have a credit history. It is essential that you have an established credit history if you are contemplating seeking outside startup capital.

Being a woman in business does have some benefits, if your business bids on Government contracts (City, County, State, Federal agencies) your bid is given priority, lending institutions also give special attention to women owned businesses.

MINORITIES

Minorities is not a very exacting term when it comes to describing the variety of groups bunched into this category, especially when it comes to business participation. Some of the minority groups that come to mind are Hispanics, which are comprised of those people from Mexico, South America, and Spain for the most part, then African Americans, Asian and Pacific Islanders and the American Indian.

Another group not really showing up on the minority radar are the Veterans. These man and woman who have served our country, no matter what war -era they were in, are more likely to follow that Entrepreneurship calling than non-veterans. The leadership and organizational training as well as the confidence provided by military service are great building blocks for starting a new business.

Minority groups have similar challenges when it comes to opening a business, the information provided in this book applies to anyone thinking of opening a business. Be aware there are numerous resources available through different Government agencies, both State and Federal, were they have special programs and grants designed just for Minorities and Woman.

And don't be afraid to contact your State and/or Federal Congressmen and Senators when looking for assistance in opening your business. The SBA and the Web are also excellent resources for information pertaining to any questions you may have for opening your new business.

The challenges Woman and Minorities face are not a whole lot different than any other person looking to open a new business, always present yourself professionally, and with confidence, show pride in whatever it is you are going to do, know everything about *your* business and be able to sing it's praises. Whether you're looking for funding, vendors or customers, presentation counts.

Your ability to communicate is also a vital part of business, whether it is your command of the English language or your ability to speak in public or write professional correspondence you must be able to converse. Frist impressions are important, you never get a second chance for a first impression. A well thought out "elevator speech" (your first 30 seconds) when you first meet someone new, gives them the opportunity to see you and your business at a glance.

Starting a new business takes on many challenges, but regardless of you gender, age or minority make up, if you have decided that you are ready to become that next business owner start getting those ducks lined up; Name it, Document it, Plan it, Finance it and GO FOR IT.

CHAPTER 10

THERE IS A CHANCE YOU COULD FAIL

DON'T FEAR FAILURE

Now that you have decided to follow that little entrepreneurial genome, and head off into business ownership, let's get past for a minute all the hype and excitement and confront that little black cloud hiding in the back of your mind, what if it doesn't work and I fail.

According to the Small Business Administration over 50% of new businesses fail with in the first year to year and a half. If you think about it that is a startling percentage, but if your cup is half full it means 50% succeed. Let's take a look at why some of those businesses fail, here are the top 5:

1. <u>Money</u> – Lack of startup capital, Failure to track finances, Overspending, Lack of reserve capital.

2. Growing too fast – can stretch capital as well as dilute your ability to perform

3. Poor Execution – Lack of leadership abilities, Poor operational structure, Lack of customer service skills.

4. Inadequate Business Plan – A poorly formatted or No plan means you have no goals, financial guidelines, or operations format.

5. Ineffective Marketing and Underestimating the Competition – Never be the best kept secret in town, and always be aware of the competition.

All of these are easily overcome with just a little pre planning on your part. As we covered in earlier chapters in this book, a business plan gives you guidelines and goals, operational procedures and financial requirements for startup capital and income expectations. These are the nuts and bolts of whether a business will succeed or fail. Let's talk a little about the not so tangible part of your business, YOU.

As a rule, Entrepreneurs tend to be "A" type personalities. They are thought of as strong minded, aggressive and focused individuals. And to some extent that is true. But if you have the passion for what you are about to start, you will find that these traits will come to the surface. Although remember you as the owner of the business, must make the decisions that will ultimately make your business grow and prosper, or not. That doesn't always mean you will be the one out front, but it will mean that it is your idea and vision that will be the determining factor in your success or failure. You will be responsible for setting Company policy, hiring, training and mentoring your staff and being the guiding light to take the company on into the future.

If you are a Sole Proprietor, keep in mind it is up to you to keep yourself disciplined, motivated and on track. Don't be afraid to have those little talks with yourself from time to time, manage your time, be aware of your financial considerations and the development of your business are all part of your responsibilities as a business owner.

Hopefully as your business grows and starts to develop you may find that even though you had a great business plan, in the business world, things have a tendency to change, and you have to have the flexibility to see it coming and react. It may be a major change or just some fine tuning, but always keep your vision and your end game in sight and be realistic and evaluative about changing anything. It must always be for the benefit of the Company as a whole. Keep in mind the success or failure of your company, especially in the beginning, is on your shoulders. If you will go back and review the top 5 reasons businesses fail and keep these in mind as you make decisions regarding your business, your chances of success will greatly improve.

Many people do not have the drive to start a business on their own but are more inclined to take over an established business one that already has the groundwork in place. If this opportunity comes up by all means get a qualified business appraiser involved. Your books are not the only thing showing your companies value, sweat equity, name recognition and your position in the industry as well as other intangibles all need to be considered and are best valued by a business appraiser professional.

It took a lot of thought, effort and planning to open your business, should you find the need to close the business, put that same effort into the closure. If none of your options seem feasible let's review some of the things you need to take into consideration when thinking about closing.

Depending on how you have structured your business, you may have to get an Attorney involved.

But if you are a Sole Proprietor it is a pretty straight forward process, the following list will help you walk away with the least amount of heart aches and headaches.

- Decided on a closing date. Giving yourself time to accomplish what needs to be done
- You will need to notify employees, vendors, suppliers and everyone you do business with of your closing date.
- If you have signed lease agreements for office or building space, equipment or other items you needed at the time to run your business, you will need to discuss your options on getting out of these leases. One of the downsides of Sole Proprietors is you generally are personally responsible for leases or loans you may have initiated during your time business don't be afraid to get some legal advice if necessary.
- You will need to cancel your Trade Name, Employer Identification Number, any Licenses, Permits or any registrations that pertain to your business.

- Financial obligations to your employees need to be paid through the closing date.

- Be sure that you ask for a final billing from all vendors and suppliers, being aware that you may be able to return inventory, which may only cost you a restocking fee.

- You will also need to pay all Federal, State and local tax agencies, I.E. payroll, sales tax and any use taxes.

- You need to be sure your records are complete and up to date. When you file your income tax for the year you closed, you may be able to write some of your expenses off, this is something you need to discuss with your account.

The closing of a business is a heartfelt and emotional experience and should not be taken to personally as there are possibly numerous reasons for the decision to close. There are many Entrepreneurs out there that have had "failed" businesses but have turned right around and started all over again, only to become successful. The second time around you will be armed with valuable information of what worked and what didn't. This will only enhance your chances of success this time around.

As an aside should you decide to go back into the workforce, most employers when looking at a resume take a "owned my own business" as a positive indication of your management and leadership abilities as well as your commitment to take on a project.

ARTHUR FOSS

AUTHORS BIO

The *One Hour Guide to:* is an ongoing series of specific topics of general interest, designed for the individual who has only so much time but still wants the information they need to better their lives. The books are written in such a format, that they should be able to be read in an hour. In today's world of instant information, the *One Hour Guide to:* is an alternative to information gathered on the web, allowing the reader to take it with them anywhere, read at their leisure, and make notes in the margins.

Arthur Foss has currently, almost retired, to Arizona with his wife of 55 years, Ellen. They have two children and a grandson. He is continuing to write other *One Hour Guide to* books such as Public Speaking, Procrastination, Salesmanship, Time Management, and Customer Service to name a few. As well as an Action/Adventure novel "Reluctant Assassin."

Drawing from his extensive background in the Military, Corporate Business, and Small Business Ownership worlds, has given him the ability to write in a humorous and common-sense fashion that allows the reader to pull from it what they need to know.